Taking the Long Way Home

May 2021

For Megan, a much-appreciated
step-mother. That does not get
said enough :)

Judy

Taking the Long Way Home

Poems by

Mary Rohrer-Dann

Cover design by Shay Culligan

ISBN: 978-1-952326-76-9

Kelsay Books
502 South 1040 East, A-119
American Fork, Utah, 84003

For my second mother

Elisabeth Lina Eisele Rohrer

who, with my father, knitted two broken families into one and gave us all childhoods where we could be fully children.

I give thanks to Michael Stephen Dann and Chelsea Elisabeth Catherine Rohrer-Dann for their love and sustaining enthusiasm for my writing, to Peggy, Diane, Betty, Eileen, and Fred, who have taken such good and often daily care of our mother and who have cheered along these poems, to Mary Shay McGuire and Carol Motta, gifted and patient readers from the very beginning, and to Sarah Russell, editor extraordinaire.

My mother is singing.
And she is going to sing.
May there be song even into twilight.

Acknowledgments

I want to acknowledge the editors of the following publications. I am grateful for their support. Some of these poems may have first appeared in a slightly different form:

Biscuit Root Drive: Grace Notes, Last Sunday in Advent, To Be of Use, Tyranny of Transitions

Flashes of Brilliance: Ode to the Orange Chairs, The Last Night in Her Home

Literary Heist: Taking the Long Way Home

MacQueen's Quinterly: Elegy for Houses

Misfit: Dementia Detail

San Antonio Review: 13 Ways of Looking at My Second Mother, Variation on a Theme, War Stories

Streetlight Press: Almost All, What My Mother Gave Me

The Atlanta Review: The winter she lies dying

The Drabble: What the Body Knows (published as Metaphor)

Vita Brevis: Morning with Beethoven, Picking Cherries

Writing in a Woman's Voice: Memories of My Father, My Mother Remembers Her Mother Praying

Contents

III

I

Glimpses of My First Mother

for Catherine Mary Tierney Rohrer

My mother's rosary pours between my fingers,
blue glass beads cascading light.
She sits beside me in her white straw hat,
murmuring responses to the Latin Mass.

I prance beside her in my new sandals,
their jaunty cut-out stars, crescent moons,
their mutinous shout of white leather.
My father said, *No white shoes,*
but we bought them anyway.

Thunder booms. Her quaking
shakes me. The windows flash
white then blue then black
then white in the night.

Defiant, I dash from kitchen to parlor.
Perhaps I poured milk on the floor, sassed back,
or pinched my baby sister. I don't remember. But oh,
the shock of my mother's hand when she catches me.

She presses us to her, reminds us
she'll be in the hospital when we come
home from school. My sister throws up.
Our mother cleans her, tucks a fresh hankie
in her fist, hugs us once more by the door,
I pull away. *You're not coming back.*
It's the last thing I say to her.

Our final day at Presentation B.V.M.
We will live with my cousin in New Jersey,
attend public school. The nun who teaches
my sister's first grade class says our mother is sick
because she married a man outside the Faith.

The winter she lies dying

for Frederick Christian Rohrer

he moves without compass—
the world buried beneath record snows,
sun wrapped in winding sheets.
        All reference points vanished.

He finishes work as others are waking,
breakfasts on beer at an all-night tavern,
then navigates home to an empty bed, empty rooms—
        the children scattered to relatives.

From bakeshop to bar to bed to hospital,
then across the Delaware, or past the cemetery
on Old York Road to visit his daughters—
        the heart's circumference a simple equation.

White afternoons, he travels
to the hospital where Christ hangs
crucified in every room, where
his life lies in a narrow steel bed.

Her soul roams an uncharted course.
He caresses fingers bloated with poisons,
seeks resurrection in fever-blind eyes,
kisses her jaundiced cheek to call her back.

If she recognizes him, he bends to her,
whispers words in German so the black-robed
crone working her beads in the corner
won't know his tenderness.

Snowy evenings, he stands the girls in the parking lot,
points through falling constellations against their forgetting.
They wave, four little nesting dolls in woolen coats,
convinced they see her in a yellow square of light.

New Year's Eve, more snow.
The doctors say, "Six weeks."
He stumbles into ghost-thick air,
knows himself a widower.
          And yet, cannot believe.

Mute before his daughters' trust
he continues into February,
hope's false courier, gathering
their crayoned talismans like roses.

He keeps what promises he can.
Two days before Valentine's,
into her coffin burdened with flowers,
he slips their paper hearts.

Logic

My mother is not dead. She lies asleep
in a little stone house at the cemetery.
When she wakes, a gardener will hear her, open
the heavy door, call my father to bring her home.
Night after night, I work out the details
of her return. She will be very hungry.
She might be mad we left her alone so long.
But she will be so happy to see us.
We will all go home together.
And she won't be sick anymore.

Hindsight

After her death, my mother's sister will find a photo
from the year before and see what no one saw then.
My mother had four children in seven years.
Everyone thought she was just tired.
By the time jaundice turned her yellow,
it was too late. She was always frail, born
at home, a month too early. Daily, her mother
measured her growth against her sister's doll.

Even Hallmark Would Pass On this Script

A fresh-off-the-boat young woman attends
a neighbor's wedding with relatives.
They lend her a matronly dress.

The groom tells his brother
You'd better catch her
before someone else does.

The groom is my father.
Ten years later, a widower,
he will follow his own advice.

Too Soon

How would you like a new mother? Dad asks.
We sit in a row on my grandmother's couch.
I am eight. My sisters are six and four and two.
I stare at the pink glass candy dish on the table.
I imagine a brassy blonde (I actually think *brassy*).
I see waxy red lipstick and scarlet nails.
No, I say. *We don't need a new mother.*

Predicament

For a long time, I don't address this new mother.
I speak to her only when we stand face to face.
I can't call her Mommy. That name is taken.
She says it's okay to call her Lina,
but I can't do that either.

Benediction

Again, I'm sent to relatives.
My new mother lies in the hospital
having my brother. I ride my bike past
a long-vacant house, glimpse movement.
My first mother stands in the open doorway.
She smiles, raises her hand.
Later, I will understand
she was waving goodbye, but for now,
something in me relaxes.
Breathes.

Attrition

The person in the coffin wears
my mother's blue dress but
the wrong lipstick and nail polish.
That's not my mother, I tell my father.
Decades later, my aunt remembers
my four-year-old sister yelling this
as she was lifted to say goodbye.
Clearly—now—these words belong
to a child much younger than I was.
I have so few memories of my mother.
Now I have one less.

Sleepwalker

My second mother often tells how I walked
in my sleep after she and Dad married.

I'd stand in the dark on her side of the bed.
Or sit on the stairs as she ironed late at night.

She would lead me back to my bed.

Once, recalling my night wanderings,
she said, *You were looking for your mother.*

Those rare times when she mentioned my first mother,
I always heard her tone of self-doubt as blame.

These words were a gift I didn't know I needed.

I think of my nine-year-old self yearning
for a face I no longer remembered clearly.

Was I keeping watch against losing this second mother, too?

Memories of My Father

I don't care if you come home crying, my dad
tells my five-year-old self. *Just make sure
the other guy is crying too.* The other guy
is also five, also named Mary.

My father throws me from his shoulders
into Sunshine Lake. I plunge into tea-
colored cedar water, rise to droplets
sliding like diamonds down his arms.

Draw five lines, he says, *any which way.*
Then he takes my crayon, sketches a face.
Again! I draw ever more haphazard, giddy lines.
Sly, surprised, silly faces crowd the paper.
Someday, my sisters and brother and I
will teach this game to our kids.

He loves telling about his days
as an Army cook, about baking
a general's favorite cake in the heaving
hold of a troopship during a typhoon,
how he had a pet monkey on Leyte,
saw village women suckling piglets
in New Guinea. Rarely, does he talk
about his regiment gearing up
to invade Tokyo.
        Then, Hiroshima.

Stop yelling at Mom, I shout at him.
His fury, all volume, vanishes like steam
but leaves the rest of us shaking.
I am the only one who yells back.

Long after he quits his Pall Malls and beer,
even after retiring, his baker's smell
of flour, sugar, and butter lingers
in the lines of his hands, the back of his neck,
his bitten-to-the-quick nails.

Eighty, my dad swings a badminton
racquet at lumbering carpenter bees
that nest in the patio roof. Every
afternoon, he and the bees perform
their inelegant *pas de deux.*

Near the end, long past midnight, Dad and I
watch the hospital meditation channel.
Molten colors flow and bloom, transform.
I kiss him goodnight. *I love you.*
        Oh, yeah?

Picking Cherries

My father lifts me to pick sour
cherries from my grandmother's tree.
His whiskers scrape against my skin.
Sugar cubes stuffed in our cheeks,
we eat straight from the dinged pail,
spit out yellow pits, bits of twig and leaf.

In this dream he is my young father,
dark-haired, muscled, laughter easy
on his lips as afternoon slips into blue
twilight with nothing more to do
than pick and eat cherries,
watch shadows purpling the green grass.

13 Ways of Looking at My Second Mother

after Wallace Stevens

1.
Lina whirls in the autumn winds.
Her father scolds, *You would laugh
if bombs were falling on your head.*
She knows Hitler offends God.
Why does laughter offend Him?

2.
Some Saturday nights, while the family sleeps,
she sits astride her youngest brother's bike,
and they ride to the next town where
they dance in mutinous bliss.

3.
She cuts off her hip-length braids
at hairdressing school, covers her head
with a blue wool cap, walks home
to her father's broad hand
hard across her face.

4.
Her mother pleads, *Don't do it,
don't do it,* but, twenty-one, she boards
the ship anyway, her mother's words
circling closer and closer down the years.

5.
To protect from icy gales, her mother sews
her a coat from a U.S. Army blanket.
The day before she leaves, a cousin brings
a hand-me-down, still-stylish, store-bought coat.
She hides the gladness piercing her.

6.
In Philadelphia, a local hairdresser
notes her skill with scissors, offers
an apprenticeship, help with earning
her license. But the aunt who sponsors her
works as a maid, insists she do the same.

7.
She marries, becomes a widow two weeks
before her daughter is born. Two years later,
she marries my widowed father, becomes
stepmother to his four little girls. With
patience, heart, tenacity, she becomes
our mother. Even mine.

8.
A silver-blue Chevy II station wagon
packed with kids, baskets of apples,
paper funnels of roasted nuts.
The sky opens. Water circles,
rising past the door handles.
My mother sings to us.

9.
The red velveteen skirt cascades
across my mother's sewing machine.
Her treadle roars long past midnight.
Tomorrow, I think, *I will be beautiful.*

10.
Which will I encounter?
The beauty of my mother's inflections,
or her razored innuendoes?
Her kinship in dreaming beyond home,
or her bitterness for all that slipped her grasp?

11.
The river is moving,
shadows crossing to and fro.
But my mother no longer flies.

12.
Her life has been one long atonement.
For defying her pious, iron-willed father.
Leaving her mother behind.
For two sisters she could not save—
dead by their own hands.
            Her riven, immigrant's heart.

13.
It is evening all afternoon.
Winter all summer long.
My mother wants to go home—
to walk across the Atlantic,
through eight decades, to Germany.

II

Arithmetic

I ask my mom why she married my dad.
You needed a mother, she says.

She had her share of proposals
from men who were not stunned with sorrow,
not blunting that sorrow with Pall Malls and beer.
But they were not men who knew how to be
a father to another man's child.

Perhaps it was a matter of simple
arithmetic. Four small girls who needed
a mother. One small girl who needed
a father. A man and woman who needed
each other. A man who needed
a friend to keep him anchored.
A woman who needed to be needed.

Here and Now

My baby brother makes
a half-dozen kids to raise.
There are meals to cook, clothes to
mend, an attic to finish, bills to pay.
Who has time or room for the past?
For grief? For ghosts who hover
in doorways and dreams?

Skinny-Dipping at Midnight

The neighborhood dark and still
under a fat orange moon,
my parents slip into silky water
when they think we are asleep.

Their soft laughter floating
through our bedroom windows,
mingling with the murmur of traffic,
tussle of leaves, still swims through my dreams.

Baking Day

My parents bicker as they bake together.
Dad likes to tease, to yell.
Mom is touchy. Her words arrow
straight to their mark.
Still, their cakes are glorious.
Zuckerkuchen, Pflaumenkuchen,
three-layer butter-cream tortes, *Stollen,*
Linzer Torte, sponge cakes with fresh apricots
like topaz glistening under golden glaze.

Being Opa and Omi

When my pregnant sister's husband suffers
catastrophic injury, my parents
parent a new way, my mother holding
my sister's hand as their first grandchild
emerges. Bringing daughter and grandson
home, they become Opa and Omi.
More grandkids follow. They change diapers,
rock babies, teach toddlers colors, games, manners,
make a front-row cheer squad at tee-ball games,
soccer matches, concerts, prom nights, graduations.
Opa teases with a new sweetness, teaches
the kids to play Uno, pinochle, and poker,
intoning, *Who dealt this mess?*
Omi sings *Hanschen Klein* to the cranky child
on her lap, and *Schlaf, Kindlein, Schlaf.*

When my daughter is born

my mother visits, a week freighted
only with joy. She sings German lullabies,
shows me how to bathe the slick pink body,
learns to be comfortable as I breastfeed.
Through stained-glass October afternoons,
we push the stroller, buy a needlepoint
kit for Chelsea's first Christmas stocking,
turn to each other, tickled, when people say
how we three—
      grandmother, mother, granddaughter
—look so much alike.

War Stories

1.

My mother and I sit at her kitchen table. Our coffee cups glow in
late afternoon light. My father, sweaty from yard work, snores in
his orange living room chair. Perhaps it is the smell of cut grass
filling the house. She tells me how French Moroccan soldiers
marched through her village after Germany surrendered. They
were given one day to do whatever they wished with the German
women and girls. Her father hid her and her sisters behind the
dovecote above the attic eaves. As she speaks, straw scrapes my
skin, dust of droppings catch in my throat. I listen for my daughter
napping in the next room.

2.

Memorial Day. Small flags line the walk. Inside, lingering over
schnapps and *apfelkuchen,* my father and his friend swap war
stories. How Hiroshima saved my father from the march on Tokyo
and certain slaughter. The horrors of the Battle of the Bulge. In
the kitchen, my sisters and I scrape plates, load the dishwasher,
gossip. My mother makes another pot of coffee, scoops whipped
cream into a clean dish, begins a story about playing truant in a
neighbor's field. A soldier found her, pulled her deeper into the
grass. My sisters and I stop laughing. Her hair hung to her hips in
straw-colored braids. She was fourteen, not yet menstruating. An
officer suddenly appeared, took my mother's hand, brought her
home to her father. I look up. My daughter stands in the doorway.
Pony-tailed, narrow-hipped, fourteen.

3.

My father has been dead nearly five years. My mother has grown old. She no longer drives. She worries someone peers in her windows at night. Her refrigerator contains only milk, butter, a few eggs, some apples, mustard. The house where my parents raised six children, where they baked together for forty-five years, where they laughed and squabbled over countless meals and games of Scrabble, is up for sale. She will move to a one-bedroom apartment that is easier to manage. There is so much to go through. So much to divide among family, give away, throw out. We take a break to run errands. It is a beautiful May afternoon. We visit the cemetery, plant snapdragons and marigolds where my father's family lies. It is something they did together. Afterwards, we drive to Walmart to buy plastic storage bins. Suddenly, in the parking lot, she returns to that day in Germany. This time, she says she was only nine or ten. From the dovecote, she and her sisters watched gaunt soldiers tear her mother's few remaining chickens apart and eat the bloody flesh. The Walmart cart my mother pushes toward the entrance steadies her. Now, in her story, she is older, thirteen or fourteen, cleaning her aunt's house. She steps outside to hang wash rags to dry. There is no soldier in a field—there are many. A ring of them. They take her to the barn. An officer appears. The officer says he will spare my mother if her older cousin, a girl of almost twenty, takes her place. The shopping cart bumps across the broken macadam. The night before, we sat in the kitchen, sorting a shoebox of old German photos. In the soft gold light, she stared at a black and white picture of a stout, middle-aged woman with wavy hair. A cousin. She spoke a name she'd never mentioned before. She sat quietly. Then she picked up another photo, blur of a child moving.

La La Girls

We call them the "La La Girls," my mother
and her *Deutsche Chorus Harmonie* friends
who laugh together like teenagers, gather
at each other's homes for *Kaffee mit Kuchen,*
lavish their tables with candles and flowers.
Their voices soar and swoop like birds,
the chance English word a flash
of iridescent green feather.

What My Mother Gave Me

The Christmas I was twelve, Herman's Hermits.
Dvorak's *New World Symphony,* Eugene Ormandy
conducting the Philadelphia Orchestra.

At thirteen, The Monkees, Copeland's *Appalachian Spring.*
At fifteen, *West Side Story, Tales from Vienna Woods.*
Afternoons, I stole away with Jethro Tull, Richie Havens.

Downstairs, my mother traveled her own secret trails—
Chopin, Mozart, Schumann—as she browned a roast,
folded wash, sewed a sea-green paisley dress for my dance.

Home permanent nights, she doused my head in foul lotions,
winched my hair in pink plastic rollers. We ate cashews
and apple slices while Gordon MacRae and Shirley Jones

sang *If I loved You* and *You'll Never Walk Alone.*

She gave me Lanza and Callas.
Later, I took her to see *Tosca, Butterfly,*
La Boheme at the Academy of Music.

I will always wish I had taken her to the Met.

Softly, through my father's fevered last days,
she kept the small radio on his dresser playing,
enfolding him in strings, horns, rolling timpani.

After, PBS kept her company—Sarah Brightman,
those velvet-voiced boys, Celtic Thunder.
Pavarotti in Rome, Madrid, San Jose.

One night, Leonard Cohen sang in his grey fedora
and shades, his gravelly voice pulsing pure male sexiness.
My mother watched him with unabashed delight.

My Mother Remembers Her Mother Praying

Once, she followed her mother out to the barn
found her kneeling in prickly straw, forehead
pressed against the cow's coarse hide, voice

muffled in the space between rib and flank.
Her mother's words a private litany of petition,
praise—and something else—something dangerous.

By then, her older brothers were taken
for Hitler's madness. Her sisters scavenged
cratered fields for radishes, turnips, potatoes.

With her younger brother, who would soon be sent
to the Russian front, she searched the ravaged henhouse
for eggs missed by starving soldiers who picked
the orchard bare, then burned it to stumps.

One afternoon, her father stood blindfolded
between the stone barn and black mouths of rifles.
Inexplicably, the rifles were lowered.

She remembers her mother in the barn, dust
motes haloing her in light. She remembers
the thick smell of manure, milk, animal heat,
the pulse of her mother holding her God to account.

The Last Night in Her Home

Her life pared,
packed into boxes,
or given away.

Time, still, to refuse the move
to the apartment her children
believe can become home.

She stands at the basement stairs,
the green linoleum floor
a dark glimmer below.

How easily she might lose
her grip on the railing,
assert her resistance.

Always, she has toiled
to please, to placate,
her life one long apology.

One last chance
to revolt, say no.
No more good girl,

obedient daughter, wife,
mother, grandmother, friend
who always says yes.

Memory rushes helter-skelter,
a broken net of pain. Again,
she denies herself, steps back.

How to say goodbye to this house

to loved rooms stenciled now with absence?
Scuffs and gouges, stripped of their histories,
just scars needing spackle and paint.

Everything gone but a few odd pieces
of furniture none of us wants.
Easier to wait outside for Goodwill.

No peace comes, only a too-full emptiness.
I pace past the fading azaleas my father planted,
clasp the chimney's familiar shoulder.

My fingertips graze each wall, read the braille
of sun-heated brick, crumbling grout.
I wish I had prayers, a rosary of thanks.

In the flowering quince, a mourning dove
considers me, her eye a bright bead.
I count four fledglings, pearly grey.

Tonight, I will tell my mother
how their soft cooing
filled the afternoon.

Morning with Beethoven

At first light, my mother shuffles
into the dark kitchen. I lie curled
under covers in the living room, breathe
in the smell of her strong coffee, listen.

Beethoven fills the apartment. Strings,
deep-throated horns, plashing cymbals.

Whatever the day might bring—news
of a friend's fall, another funeral,
anxious hunt for misplaced keys—
our morning begins in grace.

Parade

After the high-school marching band,
a stream of antique sports cars rev
their engines. A hawk-cheeked driver
tips his herringbone cap.
My mother holds his appreciative gaze.
Their white hair, luminous semaphores
of the buoyant rhythms of life.

Ode to the Orange Chairs

A sister texts the family: *Last call.*
The orange chairs go to the dumpster today.

Side by side in their orange chairs, my parents
watched *Carol Burnett, Everybody Loves Raymond,*
Dad dozing, Mom mending or knitting.

In winter's hush, they listened to Handel and Brahms,
watched snow fall beyond the glass, halo
the Dickens Village houses aglow on the wide sill.

Dad's last Thanksgiving, we gathered for a photo.
Mom leaned against him in his orange chair,
kissed his cheek. Grandkids sat at his feet.

New Year's, in his chair, his heart stopped.
Revived, he returned to us for one more month.
On Super Bowl Sunday, the hospice nurse said

Soon. Maybe a few days. A day. Tomorrow.
Two of us knelt beside our mother in her chair.
We held her hands, held her, told her

what she refused to know.

Later, she moved to a small one-bedroom.
The orange chairs, cupping memories
of home, helped make a new home

where we sat together watching old shows
mit Kaffee und Kuchen, or red wine and brie.
We paged old photo albums that kindled stories.

The stories grew darker. Bitter. Jumbled.
Another move, another winnowing.
We crammed the orange chairs into Assisted Living.

When a neighbor found her pushing her walker
in the street three blocks away, heading home
to Germany, the facility kicked her out.

We searched for another nursing home.
She shuttled between our houses.
The orange chairs moved to storage.

Now she lives in a narrow room. Narrow bed.
Narrow closet. A few family photos, her stuffed dog,
a comforter she knit in another life.

The orange chairs go to the dumpster.

III

Taking the Long Way Home

Old World rules weakened
with citizenship, marriage.
But it was the driver's license
that brought her lightness.
She explored her new country
in a red and white Ford Falcon,
white-walled tires glossy as wings.

Beneath her wheels, miles
disappeared. Years.
She lost two husbands, two homes.
Finally, her license.

She lives now behind windows
that let in light but no air.
She turns and returns
to old wounds, resentments.

But when I visit,
we go for a drive
and her rage yields
to winding roads, tunnels
of green. Burdens crumble
like the fieldstone barns tumbling
to goldenrod and chicory.

Chin raised, she is back
in the red and white Falcon,
keen to see where the road
takes her, riding it
like a hawk rides air.

Visual Aid

Nothing—not my mother's rage, confusion,
her marrow-deep sadness, the daily suck
of memory into relentless void—

nothing shocks like the image
I find online:
an Alzheimer brain beside a normal brain.

Shriveled, shrunken, it looks like a pelvis bone,
cortex and hippocampus scraped down,
cavernous holes filled with fluid.

Dementia Detail

It's just Mom and me today.

When her bedroom door opens,
I call, Good morning.
        She glares. *Nothing is good.*

I set out her breakfast.
        Don't watch me eat.
        You're always watching me.

Leave the kitchen.
        She calls after me.
        How would you like it?
        Your own children
        telling you what to do,
        whispering behind your back?

Pour a cup of coffee.
        You made it too weak again.

Ask if she wants more fruit.
        I can get it, I'm not stupid.

Time for morning meds, I say.
        None of it does any good.

How about a shower, today?
        Why? You think I'm dirty?

She reaches for the walker, shuffles to the door.
She turns and turns and turns the knob.
(Front door, back door, basement—
we've fitted all with covers.)

Finally, I say, It sticks sometimes; let me get it.
She pushes past.
You can't use the walker on the stairs, Mom.

She hurls it down the stone steps,
turns back into the kitchen.
>   *You never cared for anyone but yourself.*
>   *I'm not your mother.*
I gather the walker, bring it inside.

Eyes huge, she coils in panic.
>   *Where are my parents?*
>   *Do they know what you're doing?*

She buries her face in her hands,
sobs, shoulders quaking.
Swats away my hand.
>   *I want to go home.*

Last Sunday of Advent

My mother shrinks from touch, twisting away if I hug her, try to rub her back, turning her cheek when I seek to kiss her. But tonight, she curls into my shoulder as we sit on a small striped sofa beside a plastic Christmas tree trimmed with red and gold bows. She leans her head against my breast, lets me stroke her hand. She weeps and weeps, her words a garble of English and German.

I open a bag of tangerines, peel one for her, lay the bright crescents in a small bowl. She gobbles them down, her tears mingling with hiccups, a tremulous laugh. *Don't worry,* I say, *your parents are sitting in the garden. In Germany. It's too late to visit them now, but we'll go tomorrow, when it's light.* She cradles her plastic baby doll, its pursed, painted mouth crusted with food. I peel another tangerine, and we take turns feeding each other.

Tyranny of Transitions

At the arboretum, I peer through
a steel kaleidoscope set in a bowl
of blue and pink and orange flowers.
A dragonfly's touch, a breeze,
my own exhalation—
shifts the pattern.
Even ordinary transitions
unsettle dementia patients
and I think of Mom opening
a door, looking out a window.
Moving from one room to another.
Watching as she rides in my car
the world hurtle towards her—
then
vanishing.

Elegy for Houses

Route 611 North relaxes from clogged strip mall artery to country road curving past family farms and U-Pick orchards. Mom leans forward as she moves back in time. She has always loved driving. Long relegated to the passenger seat, on a drive, she still—sometimes—reclaims her clarity. Clarity that has dimmed relentlessly since my father died and she moved from their beloved home to an Independent Living apartment. And then, an Assisted Living studio.

But today, in the car, her eyes gleam. *Let's find Cold Spring Creamery Road!*

I know which bend in the road will reveal the house where she first worked when she came to America. There. Nestled beside a groomed pond fringed with yellow iris, a gracious summer "cottage." Wonder lights her face, as if she can see through the carved mahogany door. *It hasn't changed! I learned English here.* Through "Search for Tomorrow" and *"Guiding Light"* she acquired vocabulary and syntax as she dusted, ironed, polished old silver.

We drive on, park before a white colonial. A middle-aged man rides a mower next door. Mom rolls down her window, waves him over, something she would never have done before. Incredibly, he remembers the family she worked for, remembers the bachelor brother who lived in the carriage house. The brother eventually married and had four kids. *George? Married?* She knew him as a playboy who daily pestered her to take a spin in his Corvette convertible.

With Mom still exclaiming over George, we head into Doylestown, with its heirloom hydrangeas and rhododendrons. *Here.* She points to a grey stone house fronted with two-story-high white columns. *I scrubbed those, spring and fall. I always worried the Mister was looking up my dress.* Was he the one who wanted the coffee cake? I ask. She laughs. A novice baker, she had stirred a cup of coffee grounds into the batter. He ate a whole slice, then gently suggested she use prepared coffee next time. She smiles. *They were good people.*

We turn south towards Jenkintown, navigate winding streets. She hesitates. *There?* A red brick Cape Cod with an overgrown garden. *Yes.* Here, she kept house for an older widower. They fell in love, married. He died two weeks before their daughter was born. Before he could change his will. While she labored alone in the hospital, his born-again son-in-law changed the locks. Cradling her newborn, she returned to the house of the aunt who sponsored her emigration to America.

The sun is setting. We're both hungry. Her head nods. Tomorrow, I say, we'll go see our old house on Ryers Avenue. She turns to me tearfully. *I heard they are tearing it down.* No, Mom. The people who bought our house love it. No one is tearing it down. I'll show you tomorrow.

But the next day she is too tired. She frets, plucking at the tablecloth. The day after that, I must return to my own home four hours away. Soon, we will have no more leisurely drives. Soon, she will be so agitated and confused that my family must stop taking her for rides because she tries to open the car door in fast-moving traffic.

Like those drives, our cherished family home on Ryers Avenue vanishes into the void of Alzheimer's. The brick house with red awnings and green backyard where my widowed father and his four small girls formed a new family with my widowed stepmother. Where my stepmother became my mother. This house of boisterous parties and picnics that embraced relatives, friends, neighbors, this house is wiped from my mother's memory.

And in the torturous logic of Alzheimer's, my mother's dread of a loved house destroyed swerves to her childhood home in Diedelsheim, Germany. The thick-walled, three-story house her father built for his family of nine children is the home she now fears is gone. This is the home she yearns to return to and live in. With her mother and father.

I ask a cousin in Germany to take a photo of the house. I frame it, set it on the sill by her narrow bed on the locked floor of her nursing home where she can see it when she wakens and when she falls asleep.

What the Body Knows

Dog arrowing home.
Sunflower tracking sun.
Steel needle quivering north.
River opening to ocean.
True as any of these
my mother knows
each door's location,
senses when one opens,
is left ajar or unlocked,
when the exit alarm
two corridors down
is disarmed.

To Be of Use

My mother never knew idleness.

Long ago, she forgot how to
cast on, tie off. To beat egg,
flour, and milk for *spaetzle.*
Even how to make coffee.

Still, she smooths wrinkles
in washcloths and paper napkins.
Clears crumbs and smears
from tables. Shuffling down
the hallway, she makes a beeline
for the distant fluff of lint
or scrap of paper on the floor.

Even now, when she pleads to die,
the body's habits defeat
the desires of mind, heart.

Grace Notes

for Diane

Our mother spurns the treats we've brought,
scowls at the rain, fellow residents
dozing or moaning or yelling.
An aide mentions a Valentine's
party in the all-purpose room.

We wheel Mom through a doorway
trembling with balloons—
red and white and pink.
Heart-shaped cakes crinkle in plastic.
Coffee steams in Styrofoam cups.

At a battered baby grand a silver-haired
man sings a dappled river of songs.
I've Got My Love to Keep Me Warm.
Sentimental Journey.
Mom frowns, picks at her sweater.

You're Breaking My Heart.
Fly Me to the Moon.
Her head nods with the beat,
feet and fingers tap, eyes quicken.
Because of You. Let's Do It.

She sings softly.
Baby It's Cold Outside.
Allegheny Moon. Misty.
Insists we share the wheelchair footrest.
I Get a Kick Out of You. Night and Day.

Somewhere My Love.
She turns to my sister, then to me.
"I'm so glad you're here."
Someone to Watch Over Me.
You Belong to Me.

Almost All

A pale flower opening,
my mother's face.
She knows she knows us.
Perhaps, when we tell her
our names, remembers.
We've brought fruit, Danish,
Dunkin Donuts coffee.
   Wonderful.
Even more now, she responds best to men.
Eyes alight, chin tilted, she strokes
my husband's muscled forearm.
   You look so good! So young!
She turns, pats my cheek.
   You look good too.
Her happiness is forthright.
Fleeting.
She shudders.
Weeps and weeps and weeps.

She cannot remember all she has lost,
but knows she has lost almost all.

Thrift Store Treasure

Creamy Lenox porcelain,
gently fluted rim, slim handle
fitted for a woman's fingers,
gift from my mother one long-ago
morning as we sat at her table
and I said, *Oh! How pretty.*

In a pale wash of colors,
a yellow butterfly drifts
above blue and pink blossoms,
bumblebee and dragonfly
dart with translucent wings.
A ladybug roams a thin green stem.

Dementia has looted my mother of language,
memory, taste buds, her skilled hands.
Still, every morning, I hear her voice,
see her keen eye, feel her delight
at finding chance treasure, her pleasure
at giving, as I sip from this elegant cup.

Variation on a Theme

after W.S. Merwin

Thank you my sisters my brother my nieces who
take turns visiting each Saturday and Sunday and sometimes
a Tuesday or Wednesday evening after work
bringing her sweet milky coffee and mini donuts
or grapes and tangerines and sometimes nail scissors and
candy-colored polish and now and then one of their dogs
whose tender eyes need no look of recognition
whose velvet ears need no words of sense
thank you to the women and the men too who work for little pay
in what must be deep deep boredom
who bathe her and change her soiled clothes
who rub her hands with Nivea, her slack arms, swollen feet
who hold the spoon to her trembling mouth when she forgets
what a spoon is for, these young women with hopes for more
as they work their way through double shifts and nursing school
whose dark skin and shining hair and accented English
my mother will sometimes comment on,
and thank you to the older aides with bad knees, bad teeth,
whose backs are bent and yet they lift my mother,
dress and undress and dress her and who sometimes
when she throws her walker or raises her arm to strike
can defuse and soothe her when none of us can
(and take her blows when nothing can calm her)
and thank you for those few years when she and I
found at last an artless easy delight in each other
for our long overnight visits and drives
through Pennsylvania countryside
when memories of her German girlhood burbled up
and our leisurely mornings of coffee and music
that unlocked so many stories of her joys, regrets,
the people she loved, her sorrows and pleasures,
her pride in all she made, her brown eyes clear and warm
across the kitchen table or summer nights on the back patio
pale stars glimmering in the darkening sky.

Thanksgiving

On my morning walk, a willow leaf
dancing in air like a lure in clear water
veined gold tied to spider silk.

A briny wedge of brie
pears green and gold
dish of iced *Lebkuchen.*

Maria Callas pouring
from the radio in the kitchen
my mother, radiant.

About the Author

Mary Rohrer-Dann is a writer and painter who grew up in Philadelphia and now lives in central Pennsylvania. She taught writing and literature for many years at Pennsylvania State University. Her work has appeared in *Sun Dog, Antietam Review, Best of Philadelphia Stories Anthology 2, San Antonio Review, MacQueen's Quinterly, Flashes of Brilliance, Flash Fiction, Literary Heist,* and other publications. Two narrative poem projects, *La Scaffetta*: *Poems from the Foundling Drawer,* and *Accidents of Being,* were adapted to stage by Tempest Productions, Inc. and produced in NYC; State College, PA; and Philadelphia. She lives with her husband Michael Dann in State College, PA., and visits their daughter Chelsea (of whom she is immensely proud) in California whenever she can.

Kelsay Books

Made in the USA
Middletown, DE
21 March 2021